KT-555-940

Your First GOLDFISH

Mariana Gilbert

CONTENTS

Pages 2 and 3:
Photo by
Bob Mertlich

•
T.F.H.
Publications,
The Spinney,
Parklands,
Denmead,
Portsmouth
PO7 6AR
England

Introduction

The goldfish is undoubtedly the most popular aquarium fish in the world, so much so that it, more so than any other aquarium fish, needs no description to the average person. Most of us have kept goldfish when we were children or have at least seen them in the homes of friends. In spite of the enormous developments that have taken place in the keeping of tropical fish, the goldfish remains, along with the dog and the budgerigar, the world's senior pet. The reason for this is not difficult to understand, for the goldfish is an amazingly hardy animal that can withstand all sorts of deprivations.

HISTORY

Exactly when the goldfish was first kept in captivity by man is not known for sure, but it is generally thought that it was during the Chinese Sung dynasty (960–1279 AD). At that time *Chi-yu* (golden fish) were kept in the vicinity of temples along with the wild types from which they were bred—probably the crucian carp, *Carassius carassius*. From China, goldfish first went to Korea and by 1500 arrived in Japan, where continued selective breeding took place, producing many varieties and color variations. The first goldfish to reach Europe—as early as the 16th century—probably originated in China. By the 18th century goldfish were becoming quite widespread. Japanese fish first arrived in Europe and America during the 19th century, when at the same time hatcheries in Germany, Italy and elsewhere were being established to cope with the ever-increasing demand for these attractive and tough little fish.

Credit for the introduction of goldfish to the U.S.A. is given to Rear Admiral Daniel Ammon, who brought a consignment from the Orient that was supplied to the U.S. Fish Commission. Soon thousands of private individuals, quick to recognize the potential of goldfish, were importing stock from both the Far East and Europe. Today, the U.S.A. and Japan are the largest breeders of the many varieties of goldfish that have now become established, and the breeding of the more exotic types is now an enormous hobby as well as profession. China, the original home of the goldfish, still maintains a very strong interest in developing varieties, and breeding stations are maintained under government control.

It is hoped that this volume will enable the reader to gain far more enjoyment from his/her pet than if it were condemned, as many sadly still are, to life in that infamous prison, the goldfish bowl.

Aquariums

The desire to keep fish of many species in a glass tank, as opposed to those kept in outdoor pools, was no doubt greatly encouraged in Europe following the opening, in 1853, of the world's first public vivarium in Regent's Park Zoo, London. Today we apply the term "vivarium" to the dry or semi-dry tanks used for housing reptiles, but this was not always so. Many thousands of visitors, seeing both freshwater and marine fish alive and swimming about, were soon putting all manner of fishes into jars or any other suitable container. Alas, like the zookeepers themselves, people found that keeping fish alive for any length of time was not quite as simple as it appeared. However, even today, one still sees fish subjected to the same sort of conditions that they were in Victorian times, and none more so than the poor old goldfish.

It is not possible simply to place your goldfish in a water container, put in a few plants, and then drop in some fish flakes whenever you remember, if you expect your fish to survive well and live a happy life. That some goldfish may temporarily tolerate such conditions is not because they are surviving but because they are merely taking a long while to die! Coldwater fish need as much consideration as do tropicals, the main difference being that they do not need heated water. This simple fact believably (and also unbelievably) accounts for the casual way in which they have been treated over the years.

TANKS

In spite of the considerable knowledge available today on tank design, manufacturers still produce the traditional globular bowls with a narrow neck. These vessels have nothing to recommend them other than their cheapness. They lack a fundamental requirement, which is that of the surface area ratio of the water they contain. Fish breathe oxygen just as we do, but they extract it from water that is passed over their gill plates. The surface area of the water will largely determine the amount of oxygen that a given volume of water will contain; thus it is possible for two similar volumes to contain very different amounts of oxygen. The ideal shape of a fish tank is oblong, with the tank's length being about twice its height; this will grant a suitable surface-to-air ratio. The tank can be all glass, plastic (acrylic), or metal-framed glass. The first two are now more popular than the last named as a result of modern silicone rubber compounds that glue glass together without leaks, and the lower costs of producing molded plastic tanks,

Facing page: Full-hooded tigerhead oranda, with thick head growth on top, extending down to cover entire face. Photo by M. Gilroy. Above: Young black veiltail moor exploring its territory—better too few than too many fishes. Photo by F. Rosenzweig.

respectively. Small plastic tanks will often come complete with hoods, and thousands of beginners start off with these tanks. The drawback is that they tend to become scratched easily, and their size necessarily restricts the number of fish and plants that they can contain. As a general rule, always purchase the largest tank you can possibly afford, as it will look better, offer more potential for aquascaping, and will allow more fish to be contained in it.

FILTRATION

Theoretically, if one has a good balance between plants and fish, then the water will remain in good condition without filtration. In reality, however, this is rarely the case, and it is advisable to purchase a filter that will remove debris created by the waste of the fish, uneaten food, and dead organisms that sink to the bottom of the tank. This could be overcome by changing the water in the tank each week; however, this is both extra work and is not actually beneficial to the fish or plants, which require water that has matured—by which is meant that the water has within it the right balance of organisms and minerals conducive to good health. Your local petshop will advise you on the type of filter best suited to your aquarium needs and your family budget.

AERATION

The amount of oxygen contained in the water of the tank can be increased by the use of an air pump attached to an airstone or similar porous material. The airstone should be set near, but not on, the bottom of the tank. Goldfish require more oxygen in the water than do tropical fish, so air pumps are very useful extras; they have the further advantage that the currents they create will help to keep the temperature at a more constant level throughout the tank. Aerators will not be needed if power filters are properly fitted to and sized for the aquarium, as power filters have the same effect of disturbing the water surface, thus enhancing aeration.

LIGHT

The tank should be set where it will benefit from daylight—but not direct sunlight, which can raise the water temperature (which will reduce the amount of oxygen it contains) and increase the amount of algae growing in it, as well as increase the rate of bacterial growth. Lighting will be required for healthy plant growth, so a suitable fluorescent or tungsten light should be fitted under the tank canopy. A glass sheet should be fitted on the top of the tank to act as a condensation plate and to reduce surface evaporation of the water. Light will be required for about 12 to 14 hours daily.

TEMPERATURE

Goldfish will survive within the range of 32 to 72°F (0 to 22°C), but the most suitable range would be about 46 to 64°F (8 to 18°C). There are numerous thermometers that can be fitted either inside or outside the tank, including those stick-on strips that change colors in accordance with the water temperature. Those thermometers that are immersed in the tank water are typically the most reliable.

Goldfish kept in home tanks normally will be subjected to temperatures near the higher end of their accepted range, and that presents no problem. In fact, many of the fancier varieties of goldfish are more warmth-demanding than their more streamlined relatives. Like other aquarium fish, goldfish should not be subjected to abrupt temperature changes.

WATER

Although goldfish do not have the same need for specific water conditions as do most tropical fish, water that is neutral to slightly alkaline is probably best. A pH reading of about 7–7.5 will be required. The pH is tested by means of inexpensive kits available from your petshop or aquarist store. Likewise, the hardness of the water can be tested with kits but, given the hardiness of goldfish and the fact that you will be topping up the tank from your domestic water supply, it is probably just as well that you do not become overly fussy on this matter. Additionally, if chemicals are added wantonly to the tank water—and few of us are chemists—then serious ramifications can be the result. In essence, improperly adding chemicals to the tank can make a

small concern turn into a big problem. Tap water is often chlorinated and this is easily rendered safe simply by leaving it to stand for two to three days; an air line immersed in it to cause turbulence will speed the process— another good reason for fitting an aerator to your aquarium.

GRAVEL

You will need a layer of gravel in your tank to provide a growing medium for the plants and to anchor them firmly in place. This is important with goldfish as they enjoy rooting about at the tank bottom in search of food. Goldfish will also nibble at plants, but it is worth persevering to establish a good plant growth. The gravel should be of medium to dark colors for best effect, and about 3 mm in size. Some people prefer the brightly colored, even neon-colored, gravel, and such preference is their prerogative. Before the gravel is placed into the tank, it should first be placed in a bucket and flushed thoroughly with a current from a hose. The gravel should be forcefully disturbed periodically throughout this process; when the water runs clear from the bucket, despite the most forceful stirring, the gravel is then ready to be placed into the tank.

ROCKS

The most suitable rocks for the aquarium are granite, slate, and sandstone, although many rocks found in the natural state in water courses can be used, provided that

Above: Red and white Japanese ryukin displaying its attractive coloration. Photo by F. Rosenzweig. Facing page: Two rare calico ranchu photographed by B. Kahl. The head growths on these animals are weak, but the coloration is very good.

they are free of contaminants and do not have the chemical property to greatly raise or lower the pH of the tank—see your petshop proprietor if in doubt on the suitable nature of any given rock. Avoid all rocks with sharp edges and those such as marble, limestone, and also soft sandstone. These rocks will contain a high mineral content that will slowly leach out and make the water far too alkaline for fish and plants. Driftwood is also a useful material for landscaping the aquarium. Driftwood can be purchased at most petshops.

PLANTS

There are a number of plants that are suitable for the coldwater aquarium, and many of these are the same plants suitable for the garden pond—a fact that may well increase your plant selection when you are shopping. Select only healthy looking specimens, and always wash plants thoroughly before introducing them into your tank. Plants not only look nice but provide hiding places for the fish, sites for egglaying, and a browsing area, which is an important therapeutic aspect often overlooked by those who merely place a few rocks in a bowl with goldfish. There are many plastic plants sold these days; many are terrible but some are very lifelike and can be used to good effect as background props. I prefer the real plants but have seen artificial ones that were used extremely effectively.

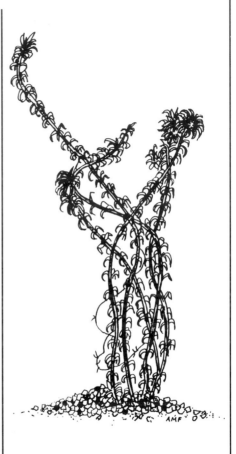

Elodea nutalli, a temperate and sub-tropical plant, originated in North America but has become naturalized in Germany and the Netherlands. It is well suited for most goldfish ponds and aquariums.

Aquascaping

The term aquascaping is used to describe the process of preparing the overall decoration of the aquarium. Obviously, there is no limit to the ways in which an aquarium can be arranged; this can vary from very formal, sparsely planted scenes, through well-planted, well-stocked views, to the more bizarre form of thematic aquascaping where a topic is selected and the tank furnished accordingly, e.g., sunken cities, galleons, fairyland and the like. While purists may frown on thematic aquascaping on the grounds that the scenes are unnatural, it must be remembered that the goldfish itself is an unnatural variety, and, more importantly, children often enjoy these types of scenes—and I believe if it encourages an interest in fishkeeping, then it is to be applauded.

SETTING UP THE AQUARIUM

Having purchased your tank and all the needed accessories, now comes the job of preparing the aquarium for the goldfish. First, before setting anything in the tank, you should draw various plans in order to see how you think your arrangement will look, giving due consideration to the height of plants, areas left for free-swimming, the best layout for rocks, and so on. A point of note here is that there are essentially two roads to travel at this point: you can either strive for an informal setting in which the contents of the tank are set up randomly (with common sense applied, of course) or you can attempt a formal setting in which the contents are set up in neat rows and with left-right balance keenly in mind. The author prefers an informal layout rather than a formal one, as an informal layout better replicates a natural setting.

Allowing for the weight of the final setup (water, rocks, gravel, etc.), the tank must be set on a solid base. It is recommended that you place a thick layer of polystyrene under the tank to even out any minor irregularities in the site surface, thus ensuring that the tank is set level and that there is an equal distribution of the weight of the tank. Avoid placing the tank opposite a door where drafts may effect a change in water temperature—which is not good for plants and fish.

Next, place the gravel and rocks into the tank and arrange them so that there is a slope from the back of the tank to the front—say 1 inch (2.5 cm) in front to 4 inches (10 cm) at the rear. Alternatively, you could build a small terrace wall across part of the tank length, about midway back, to raise the level and provide a free-swimming area in the foreground; a piece of driftwood purchased from a petshop could be used to the same effect. Rocks should be placed so they can be seen but without becoming the focal point, and they should be pushed into the gravel so that they look natural. Also at this stage, if an airstone is to be used, the airline can be neatly hidden under the gravel and the airstone tucked behind a rock. Do not hide the airstone too well, however, for it will require frequent cleaning. Remember that airstones easily become clogged.

Below: Red and white long-tailed pearlscale photographed by F. Rosenzweig. Top right: Two excellent quality red and white ryukins photographed by B. Kahl. Bottom right: Two attractive black orandas photographed by F. Rosenzweig.

ADDING THE WATER

Assuming everything looks as you want it, the water can be added by pouring it gently onto a concave plate or onto glass held at an angle and over a sheet of paper that covers the gravel, which will keep the gravel from being disturbed unduly. Fill to half way and ensure that the temperature is appropriate before planting.

The plants can be securely inserted into the substrate either with one of the special tools available for the purpose or with your fingers. Once the plants are set to your satisfaction, then the rest of the water can be added to about 2 inches (5 cm.) from the top of the tank. A strip of black tape placed lengthwise along the top of the tank will hide the waterline for better effect, if desired. Now the tank hood can be set in place and the electricity switched on to test that all is working.

It is best to leave the tank alone and running for at least three days so that the water has time to mature and, after this, siphon off any debris that may have collected at the top of the tank; also remove and replace about half of the water. Then wait another few days just to see that the plants are remaining healthy and are well anchored before adding the fish.

ADDING THE GOLDFISH

The final piece in your aquascene is, of course, the actual goldfish. Ideally, they will have been quarantined by you in a small holding tank to see that they were both feeding well and remaining in good health. If you do not quarantine, then ensure that you purchase from a reputable source. The plastic bag in which they were transported should be floated in the tank for about 20 minutes so that the temperature in it equates with that of the tank. During this time an amount of the tank water can be added to that of the container; thus the fish have the chance to accustom themselves to different water qualities. Finally, open the container gently to allow the fish to swim off and explore their new home.

MAINTENANCE

Your aquarium should be cleaned regularly, say every third week, during which time the electrical equipment should be turned off and the plugs taken from their sockets to guard against any damage or unnecessary danger. Equipment should be checked for wear, pumps serviced, and so on. It is advisable that tap water is always left to stand for a few days prior to tank cleaning—and ideally in the same room as the aquarium so temperatures are the same. At cleaning time, replace about 50–60% of the water, but not all, as this will ensure that an amount of microorganisms beneficial to the tank are retained.

A well-balanced aquarium will give you much pleasure, and the routine upkeep is probably less than that for any other pet.

Feeding

The goldfish is an omnivorous feeder, by which is meant it eats both vegetable and animal foods.

They will also eat at all levels of the water and so are most obliging and easily catered. The feeding of fish has developed considerably over the years, and today there is no shortage of every possible type of nutrient that your goldfish will need.

NUTRITIONAL REQUIREMENTS

The basic constituents of food are carbohydrates, which provide energy for muscular activity; fats, which provide insulation and reserves of energy, and assist in the absorption of vitamins; and proteins, which provide the raw material for tissue and muscle construction. Additionally, protein can be converted into carbohydrate matter when fat levels have been used up; thus, a starving animal becomes "skin and bone," as protein is the only foodstuff from which tissue can be constructed and is the last level of the energy reserves. Beyond these three major constituents, animals need vitamins of approximately 22 types, and minerals in varying amounts. These last two items are required to assist in the various metabolic processes and to build up resistance against disease. It should

be pointed out, given the amount of multi-vitamins and mineral supplements produced today, that if your fish are supplied with a balanced diet, then these additives not only will not be needed but may actually be harmful to them. Excess vitamins and minerals must be excreted by the fish but some of the material will actually be laid down in bodily tissue where it will upset normal healthy balances, and thus create problems.

The prime sources of these various constituents are vegetable matter, animal products, cereals, and dissolved minerals in the water itself. Vegetable matter is an excellent source of carbohydrates and vitamins. Vegetables also contain varying amounts of protein but are deficient in certain essential amino acids (from which protein is made), and so livefood is needed; further, vegetable protein is not assimilated as readily as animal protein, thus the need to supply a varied diet at all times. During the breeding period, fish need increased amounts of protein, whereas during the non-breeding period they need food more conducive to providing energy for muscular activity. During the winter period (in ponds) when temperatures fall to zero, fish need no food at all and will live on their fat reserves until the spring, provided that they were fed well during the warmer months.

Opposite: Full-hooded calico oranda with blue/silver coloration. *Above:* Bronze oranda contentedly roaming its swimming grounds. *Below:* Black oranda displaying its full hood and tail finnage, with the whitish growth on the tips of the tail marking new fin development. Photos by F. Rosenzweig.

FEEDING METHODS

The choice of feeding method for the modern aquarist is varied, as is the food itself, which is available as flakes, tablets, pellets, cubes, fresh, freeze-dried and deep frozen.

Commercial foods are carefully formulated to contain all the needed constituents already discussed, and a visit to a good aquarist store or petshop will reveal the vast range available to you. Flakes are very popular with goldfish keepers because they will float for quite some time before slowly sinking, thus giving the fish ample time to feed on them.

Beyond branded foods, it is strongly recommended that you also feed a varied selection of other nutrients so as to ensure good color and healthy growth in your fish.

Vegetables, such as carrots, spinach, celery and peas, can be finely shredded, as can various meats, including poultry and fish. Scrambled egg, cheese and dog chow are other possible additions to the weekly menu, while earthworms, whiteworms, daphnia, cyclops, flies (swatted—not sprayed!) woodlice and many other forms of livefood can be collected or purchased from your local supplier and fed to your fish.

Tubifex, a small worm found in sewage, is an excellent livefood, but collecting it is messy; the worms need careful washing to remove unwanted organisms. Tubifex can be purchased freeze-dried, however. The important thing is to experiment across as wide a range of foods as possible and to try to avoid becoming predictable in your feeding regimen when applied to food types.

WHEN TO FEED

The mistake made by most people when they first keep fish is that they always over-feed them. Your goldfish should only be given as much food as they can consume in two to three minutes.

Uneaten food will simply fall to the bottom of the tank, where it will decompose and add potentially harmful waste products to the water, which will eventually become cloudy through saturation of excess products.

Under normal conditions, a small feeding three times daily is sufficient and, at such times, always check that each fish is feeding.

WHEN ON VACATION

When you go on vacation, it is not necessary to have friends feed your fish; they will survive quite well for up to two weeks without food, assuming they are in fit and healthy condition. If you are away for longer periods then either get another experienced fishkeeper to attend to your pets or leave small amounts in packets with strict instructions as to when to feed—and put less-than-normal quantities in the packets just to be on the safe side.

To recap feeding: plenty of variety in small but regular amounts.

Varieties

Over many centuries of careful selective breeding of mutational forms, the common goldfish (*Carassius auratus*) has produced a great number of varieties. It is estimated that well over 100 forms are now available, though many of these in my opinion are quite grotesque (I find it difficult to understand how their breeding can be justified on either esthetic or practical grounds). However, a number show only more acceptable modifications to the normal goldfish we all know so well, and it is these with which the average person will most likely commence. It must always be remembered that the farther one diverges from the natural state, the more difficult will be the keeping of the animal in question. If you plan to keep goldfish in a garden pond, it is recommended that you restrict yourself to the more "normal" varieties that do not exhibit unusual finnage or head growths, as such varieties tend to be much more delicate—apart from which they are seen at their best in the aquarium.

THE COMMON GOLDFISH

The archetypal goldfish is of classic fish appearance, having paired pectoral and pelvic (or ventral) fins, which are used for balance, braking, turning and slow speed browsing movements. The single anal fin is largely for stabilization purposes; the caudal or tail fin is the main source of propulsion and turning, in conjunction with body movements. The large dorsal fin prevents body roll and is thus a stabilizing fin. Along the mid-line of the fish is a lateral line which is a collection of sensory cells which respond to vibrations in the water.

From this basic "model" all varieties have been developed. The multi-finned varieties, such as the veiltail, have less strong fin rays so are slower-moving than those such as the common goldfish, comet, and those with more traditional fins.

COLORS

Goldfish are available in a wide range of colors, including orange, yellow, silver, and black, together with many combinations of these colors to create the appearance of blue, red, and even brown. The controlling factor over this range of colors is the reflective layer of tissue known as iridocytes. If this is present as in normal fish then the scales are described as being *metallic*. If the upper layer of this is missing, the effect is termed *nacreous*, giving a mother-of-pearl appearance and a greater range of colors because pigment lower in the body tissue is visible. If the reflective layer is missing altogether, then the effect is

Orange/red lionhead going through a color change: all the brown markings of this fish will eventually fade to orange. Such fading is common to many varieties of goldfish. Photo by M. Gilroy.

Above: This blue oranda demonstrates well that blue orandas have little to no head growth. Below: Red and white oranda showing nice conformation. Long fins are susceptible to nips from other fishes, which necessitates consideration when selecting tank mates for orandas and some other goldfish.

called *matt*, designating no shine to the scales. It is, however, possible for some reflective tissue to be retained in an otherwise lacking fish, which gives a few shiny scales—but these are undesirable from a purist's view.

VARIETIES

As stated earlier in this chapter, there are believably over 100 goldfish varieties, many of which are not uncommon, and some of which the author feels are of dubious merit. Presented here are some of the most common varieties of the goldfish.

Comet

Developed in the U.S.A., this is a hardy, very streamlined fish in which the tail is as long as the body and deeply forked. It needs plenty of swimming space. Yellow is often its color but orange is another popular color. Metallic reflective group.

Shubunkin

Two varieties are available, the London and the Bristol. Again, these are streamlined fish with a large lobed caudal fin and an enlarged dorsal fin. They are of the nacreous group and so exhibit a whole range of colors. Like the comet, they are hardy and well suited to the outdoor pond.

Fantail

In this variety, the body is shorter than in the common goldfish, giving an egg shape. The dorsal fin is tall and the anal and caudal fins are double. Both metallic and nacreous types are available in a wide range of colors. The variety is hardy and suitable for tank or pond. In Japan the equivalent type is known as the *ryukin* and is extremely popular. A telescope-eyed version is also available.

Nymph

This is a sort of the fantail in which the anal and caudal fins remain single.

Veiltail

Somewhat larger than the fantail, the veiltail is very popular due to its long flowing fins, which are doubled as in the fantail. The body is more spherical and metallic, and nacreous forms are available in a wide range of colors. There is also a telescope-eyed variety. Although they are reasonably hardy, these fish are better suited to the aquarium than the garden pond, for there is always more risk of fin damage in the pond situation.

Oranda

This variety was developed by crossing the lionhead with the veiltail to produce a fish showing the body features of the veiltail with the characteristic hood of the lionhead. Various colors are available, including the redcap oranda in which the body is silver while the warty headgrowth is red, though this tends to fade with age.

Lionhead

In this variety, warty raspberry-like growths on the head are the obvious distinguishing feature, in addition to the lack of a dorsal fin, which means they are less stable swimmers. In Japan these fish are termed *ranchu* and are very highly prized. Lionheads have a double caudal fin and, ideally, the hood should occur evenly around the head, but specimens exhibiting excellence in this quality are not common and will be expensive. The type is metallic. Well-aerated water is needed in order that the fish can breathe through their inflexible gill plates caused by the hood. It will take about two years for the hood to develop fully.

Black Moors

This is an all-black veiltail with telescope eyes, by which is meant that the eyes are on the end of the fleshy growth. These "telescopes" take two to three years to develop fully. This fish is of the metallic scale type. Ideally, it should be black all over, but often—and with age—a bronze hue will appear on the underside and the fins. This variety is very popular in the U.S.A. and Great Britain, where it is bred to a high standard for competition.

Chinese Varieties

The more exotic goldfish are usually of Chinese origin, where the unusual or the dragon-like shapes are characteristic.

The **celestial** (metallic and nacreous) has telescope eyes that are turned upward—it is said so that they can gaze at emperors. More care will be needed in the feeding of this fish because of its restricted vision. It has no dorsal fin.

The **bubble-eye** also lacks a dorsal fin, but its most distinguishing characteristic is the fluid-filled sacs below the eyes, giving the fish a most bizarre appearance. The bubble-eye will need a carefully arranged aquarium free from any sharp projections. It is not recommended for beginners.

The **pompon** has fleshy narial septa (between the nostrils) much enlarged to form lobes known as narial bouquets. These can become very large in some specimens, and the variety may or may not have a dorsal fin. Body shape is as for the oranda.

The **pearlscale** is another unusual variety. In this variety, the scales are silver with red, and due to their raised centers give a pearl-like sheen, and their abdomens droop to give them a somewhat fat look.

There is even a tailless goldfish, which is known as the **meteor**, and many other varieties that will be seen from time to time in petshops and the hands of avid fanciers. However, the most common varieties, many of which are also the best varieties for beginners, have been discussed in this chapter.

Above: One of the more exotic goldfish, this red and white lionhead exhibits the qualities of plumpness, minimal tail finnage, and lack of dorsal fin. Below: This very attractive calico oranda won first place in its class in Akron, Ohio, 1987. Photos by F. Rosenzweig. Facing page: Two good quality celestials. The celestial originated in China, where it was selectively bred to "gaze at emperors." Photo by B. Kahl.

Breeding

The most interesting aspect of the hobby, perhaps, is breeding your goldfish, and anyone who wishes to exhibit his/her fish, or simply to produce his/her own stock, is strongly recommended to purchase one of the more detailed books published by T.F.H.—either on breeding in general or on goldfish specifically. In a book of this nature we can but look at the basic facts.

BREEDING METHODS

Some fishes, such as the very popular guppy, give birth to free-swimming young and thus are called livebearers. However, much the greater number of species reproduce by laying eggs, and thus are termed egglayers. As you may already know, the goldfish is one such egglaying species. Egglayers are conveniently divided into groups according to the way in which their eggs are laid. Loosely considered, these groups include: scatterers, substrate spawners, nestbuilders, buriers, and mouthbrooders. Goldfish are egg scatterers, which means they lay eggs quite indiscriminately and show no interest in them once laid—other than to eat them! In the wild such eggs would fall into the river beds or would stick to plants, rocks or any other surface and thus gain a measure of protection from the parents—some would be swept a distance away by the current. In the confines of an aquarium, we must therefore protect the eggs from the parents by various means.

SEXING

Egglaying fish are difficult to sex; but, as the spawning period approaches, the female will appear swollen in the abdominal region in a somewhat uneven manner, when viewed from above. This swelling is due to the eggs. The male will develop small white spots known as tubercles on the gill plates, head and pectoral fins.

BREEDING PREPARATION

First, it is essential that we breed only fully fit goldfish demonstrating excellent color as well as body shape and finnage. It is very impractical to attempt breeding in a community tank for two primary reasons: first, you will have to exert great effort to control partners; and second, the eggs stand little chance of maturing into young fry. A single breeding tank will be the absolute minimum requirement, but really two or more extra tanks should be utilized, considering that the fry will need separating and grading as they grow.

The breeding tank should be as large as possible and contain water of the same temperature as that of the main tank in which the breeding pair were living. The temperature should be increased by 3 to 5°F (2 to 3°C) once the partners are acclimated to it. A glass divider can be inserted so that the goldfish can see each other, but otherwise introduce the male first and the female a day or so later. The only tank furnishings needed are a spawning mop or some plants such as *Elodea*, though a nylon mop typically proves better. Neither gravel nor other substrate is needed, but the use of marbles will safeguard any eggs that fall to the tank bottom.

SPAWNING

The actual reproductive cycle commences with the fish's chasing each other around the tank; however, ultimately it will be the male who by prodding the female's vent induces her to shed her eggs. He will fertilize these with his sperm, known as milt. The process will be repeated until all the female's eggs are shed. If the pair fail to "mate" after being placed together, try raising the water temperature another couple of degrees. It is usual to site a breeding tank where it will catch the early morning rays of the sun, which often stimulates breeding.

RAISING THE FRY

Once the eggs are shed, the adults should be removed; otherwise you will have very few youngsters. Initially, the fish fry will obtain food by absorption of their yolk sac, but after about three to four days the fry will need food. Keep your eye on the

yolk sac so you know exactly when to start feeding. Cultures of infusoria, which are collections of microscopic organisms, and algae, which are unicellular plants, are good starter foods. The former are prepared by inserting some chopped straw, lettuce leaves or banana skin (bruised) in a jar containing boiled water and then leaving this in a warm room for a few days, after which the water will be cloudy with infusoria; a few drops can be added to the tank regularly each day for the fry. Alternatively, the jar can be placed higher than the tank and a plastic tube used to siphon into the fry's tank. A clamp should be applied to control the flow so that it is reduced to a steady very slow drip.

Algae are prepared simply by placing a jar of clean water in direct sunlight: it will soon become green with algal growth. It is possible to get infusoria tablets from your aquarist suppliers, who will also be able to supply brine shrimp eggs which can be hatched to provide live food.

SELECTION

As the young goldfish start to grow you must be quite ruthless in culling out any which are deformed or in other ways not up to standard. They can be placed in your adult stock tank and will soon be eaten, which is by far the most humane method of disposing of them. When the required young fish attain a reasonable size, they can be introduced to your community tank.

Above: Two common fantails captured in the act of spawning by photographer Jaroslav Elias. Once you have mastered the practice of keeping goldfish, you may well want to try your hand at breeding them. *Below:* A sleek comet with a long singular caudal fin. *Facing page:* Frontal view of a Chinese Lionhead. Photos by M. Gilroy.

Ailments

Your goldfish may suffer from a great range of ailments, most of which are the result of inadequacies in their accommodations, care and maintenance. As in most all aspects of life, prevention is better than cure. (We can probably all remember the cliché about an ounce of something equaling a pound of something else?) The following points should be regarded as essential husbandry.

Never introduce newly acquired fish, plants, rocks or other materials or life forms into the established tank until such material has either been subjected to a period of quarantine or thoroughly washed—according, of course, to the nature of the material. If this is not done, you risk introducing disease, predators, harmful chemicals or other similar and unwanted additions to the tank. For this reason at least one small isolation tank is a sound investment.

Always try to identify the cause of an illness before attempting to treat a given problem. Mistreating a condition or disease is often worse than not treating the condition at all, and many of the "cure-all" type medications rarely work well.

Ensure that the filtration and aeration systems are checked on a regular basis. The condition of the water, which should always look clear, is a most important factor to the health of our fish.

If you merely top up your tank with small amounts of water, chemical prostration might occur. Chemical prostration refers to the situation in which a build-up of undesirable chemicals results, for while the water evaporates, the chemicals do not and will eventually reach excessive levels. As a general rule, every three weeks about 60% of the water should be changed.

Do not overfeed, as uneaten food simply goes bad, thus contaminating the tank water.

Be sure that the aquarium is not set in such a location that it will be

Goldfish gasping for air at the surface of one of those infamous prisons—the stifling goldfish bowl.

subjected to constant variations in water temperature—such as in direct sunlight or near a drafty door or window. Constantly fluctuating temperatures create stress for the animals and can easily lead to weakness, illness and even death.

Never attempt to accommodate more goldfish than the tank will allow. Fewer but fitter fish is a much more desirable condition than an overcrowded tank: those few extra fish can put the entire tank at risk.

Illness in any animal is not difficult to spot, and, in fish, any which are not feeding as normal must be watched carefully for further signs of regression. Any fish that seems to be having difficulty in swimming or is swimming at an angle is obviously ailing. Those with bulging eyes, compared to their normal state, and those which are rubbing against stones or have growths of any kind on their scales are further examples of unhealthy goldfish and should be netted with care and placed in an isolation tank containing only water. In such an environment the fish is free of stress, and medication appropriate to the symptoms can be given without affecting the healthy members of the fish community.

T.F.H. produces a number of books on fish diseases and these are recommended to give you insight into the many likely problems and the best course of action to take. Once an illness has been identified, correctional steps as to its source should be taken with the main stock tank to ensure that it does not recur.

Bibliography

THE ABC'S OF GOLDFISH
By Neal Teitler
ISBN 0-86622-763-6
KW-153
Audience: Anyone with an interest in goldfish will benefit greatly from this book. Written by a foremost fancier, it combines plenty of information about keeping and breeding goldfish with an in-depth discussion of their many shapes and color patterns.
Hardcover, 5½ x 8", 96 pages
58 full-color photos

GOLDFISH AS A NEW PET
By Anmarie Barrie
ISBN 0-86622-606-0
TU-001
Here is an inexpensive softcover book that can be highly recommended to first-time goldfish buyers. Bright and breezy, this book makes it easy . . . loaded with good full-color photos, too.
Softcover, 7 x 8½", 64 pages

GOLDFISH AND KOI IN YOUR HOME
By Dr. Herbert R. Axelrod and William Vorderwinkler
ISBN 0-86622-636-2
TFH H-909
Contents: What Your Goldfish Need. Setting Up The Aquarium And Choosing The Plants. How To Choose Goldfish. Goldfish Varieties. How To Breed Goldfish. How To Raise Quality Goldfish. Goldfish Diseases. The Garden Pool.
Audience: For the home aquarium and tropical fish hobbyist. This book contains complete data on care and feeding, treatment of fish diseases, water conditions, and everything necessary for the home owner of goldfish and koi. Ages 13 and above.
Hard cover, 5½ x 8", 208 pages
91 black and white photos, 125 color photos